Railway Co Mexican Central

Facts And Figures About Mexico And Her Great Railroad

Railway Co Mexican Central

Facts And Figures About Mexico And Her Great Railroad

ISBN/EAN: 9783744725347

Printed in Europe, USA, Canada, Australia, Japan

Cover: Foto ©ninafisch / pixelio.de

More available books at **www.hansebooks.com**

FACTS AND FIGURES ABOUT MEXICO

AND HER GREAT RAILROAD

THE MEXICAN CENTRAL

"The old order changeth, yielding place to new" — TENNYSON

COMPLIMENTS OF

THE MEXICAN CENTRAL RAILWAY COMPANY

ISSUED BY THE BUREAU OF INFORMATION
OF
THE MEXICAN CENTRAL RAILWAY COMPANY, LIMITED
CITY OF MEXICO, MEXICO
1897

MEXICO

OFFERS TO THE SETTLER

A DELIGHTFUL CLIMATE; PARTICULARLY FAVORABLE TO THOSE WHO SUFFER FROM THE RIGORS OF A NORTHERN WINTER.

FERTILE FARMS; NONE BETTER IN THE WORLD.
A RAPIDLY DEVELOPING COUNTRY, WHERE ENERGY AND ABILITY REAP THEIR JUST REWARD.
MINING REGIONS; THE RICHEST ON THE GLOBE.
PERFECT SECURITY FOR PERSON AND PROPERTY.

A VARIETY OF MINERAL AND VEGETABLE PRODUCTIONS SUCH AS NO OTHER COUNTRY CAN EQUAL.
UNCULTIVATED LANDS OF GREAT FERTILITY.
TRANSPORTATION FACILITIES OF THE FIRST ORDER.
PLENTY OF CHEAP LABOR.

IN MEXICO THERE ARE NOW GOOD THINGS TO BE OBTAINED, WHICH UNTIL NOW COULD NOT BE OBTAINED. IN MORE DEVELOPED COUNTRIES, THE GOOD THINGS HAVE ALREADY BEEN TAKEN UP BY PEOPLE WHO PROPOSE TO KEEP THEM.

"The tide is setting south; take it at the flood."

FACTS AND FIGURES
ABOUT MEXICO

THE primary purpose of this book is to furnish answers to many of the letters which have come to the Bureau of Information, inquiring about opportunities for investment and for settlement in Mexico.

A secondary and incidental purpose is to give a glimpse of the many interesting features of the country, which are amply worthy the attention of the student and of the tourits. Here, then, we address ourselves chiefly to those who may wish to know how and where to make a home and get a living in Mexico; or may wish to know where and how without residing constantly in the country, they may make money, in Mexico.

The inquiries that reach us are: " What opportunity for 'getting ahead' does Mexico offer to the farmer of moderate means? What chance is there for a mechanic, who, besides a knowledge of his trade, has but a small capital? Is life well guarded in the country? Are titles to land beyond question? Are taxes reasonable? Is labor plenty and efficient? Is property carefully protected by just laws, and are the laws justly administered to foreigner and native alike? Where are the best opportunities to be found for money-making in trade, in mining, in general agriculture? Where are the best regions for the culture of oranges, bananas, coffee, sugar and cotton? What are the facilities for transportation? What is the condition of the country in respect to freedom in religion and schools?

These and kindred questions we attempt to answer more or less fully in this book. We know that it is the business of a "bureau of information" to inform; but we know also that there is a limit to its ability, however great its willingness, to inform.

We can and do give here much *general* information, and some that is quite specific; enough to awaken interest in the minds of any one who may wish to better his condition, or to make a venture with a hope and expectation of improving his fortune. We aim to state simply *facts* which can be verified by any one who may care to investigate; and we refrain from giving *advice* as to whether the inquirer (or the reader) had better make a venture in Mexico. What any one shall do in any given case is a matter for personal decision, when the facts in the case are presented. We do say, however, most emphatically (and with the greatest confidence that we are saying something worth heeding) that extraordinary opportunities are just now offered to those who wish to make a venture in Mexico; opportunities worthy the most careful consideration of the home-seeker who desires a mild climate with a comfortable living, and of the capitalist who wishes a quick and large return from his investment.

A NEW WORLD.

THE Mexico of to-day is a new world. It must be admitted that the reputation of the old for safety and stability was bad, very bad. But reform has been abroad in the land, and within the last thirty years a silent and salutary revolution has occurred in Mexico. This reformation is the wonder of the century to every one who has given it attention. On this point we are glad to be able to cite the testimony of a competent authority, who has recently given the result of his careful study of Mexico to the readers of *Harper's Magazine*, and we commend his articles (beginning in February, 1897,) to our readers. Mr. Lummis, under the title of "The Awakening of a Nation," aptly calls Mexico "an ambitious marcher in the procession of nations," and says:

She is no longer old Mexico; while in the United States we have been achieving a material development, she has wrought the political and social miracle of the century. Within less time than has elapsed since our Civil War invented millionaires, Mexico has stepped across as wide a gulf. From a state of anarchy tempered by brigandage, she has graduated to the most compact and unified nation in the New World. She has acquired not only a government which governs, but one which knows how to govern, and, contemporaneously, a people which has learned how to be ruled. Only those who seriously knew the country in the old days can at all conceive the change from the Mexico of a generation back to the Mexico of now. There was no touring then, and nowhere was travel more unsafe. By every country road, even into the very heart of cities, the *bandido* robbed and murdered. There were even lady Turpins, and some of them were geniuses. There were no railroads, no telegraphs, practically no commerce; at the bottom of all, no security. To-day Mexico is — and I say it deliberately — the safest country in America. Life, property, human rights are even more secure than with us. As for stability, the record speaks for itself. Mexico had sixty-two viceroys in 286 years — not very tumultuous; but it also has had fifty-two presidents, emperors, and other heads in fifty-nine years of this century. Now, one president for twenty years. Some will say that this is not republican. Possibly not, but it is business. Among all the mistakes of foreigners as to Mexico, none is more groping than that which disparages its government. I do not know anything in history which fairly parallels these twenty years in Mexico. It is not far to remember when there was not a railroad in Mexico, and when other material conditions were in proportion. The actual Mexico has forty railroads, with nearly seven thousand miles of track, and everything that that implies. Its transportation facilities are practically as good as those of our Western States, and the investment is far more profitable. It is netted with telegraph lines (with the cheapest tariff in America), dotted with post-offices, schools, costly buildings for public business, and public beneficence. It is freer than it was ever before, with free schools, free speech, free press. There is progress everywhere — material, intellectual, moral.

The sentences above quoted answer a number of the inquiries before mentioned. Mr. Lummis's statements are within bounds of truth, and are abundantly confirmed by all who are familiar with the recent history of the country. Because of these facts we are safe in saying that the Mexico of to-day is socially, politically and commercially " a new world." Into this progressive and well-protected country, favored with soil and climate unequalled, and under its new regime, for the first time able to offer small tracts of land to purchasers, to guarantee safety to all, and to assure to all equality before the law, foreigners may now come with the utmost degree of confidence and hope.

EASY ENOUGH.

THE difficulties which American settlers might at first think almost insuperable (for instance such as the difference in language and customs) will be found, on trial, to be largely imaginary. The settler will very soon and very easily acquire a workable knowledge of the Spanish, and the native will quickly learn all that he needs of the English language. The present generation of children is at work already upon the English. " In every public school of Mexico above the primary grade, in every private school, training school, and college, English is a compulsory study — in another generation," says Mr. Lummis, " Mexico is going to be equipped for business and pleasure in two languages."

The difficulties and sacrifices in the way of any one who may contemplate going to Mexico to live, are nothing compared with those which our ancestors (and even our contemporaries) encountered in making their venture in *their* "new world." When we consider the facilities available to-day, the fact that the settler in Mexico has a climate which is never severe either in heat or cold; the fact that no lurking savage foe threatens danger or death; and further, the fact that the people among whom he goes welcome him and work for and with him to bring quick results, we can but think that the American will find in Mexico infinitely more pleasant and hopeful conditions than the American of forty years ago found in Kansas and Nebraska. But the pioneers of those states thought it worth while to make a move from the crowded or worn-out regions of the eastern United States, and have found their reward in prosperity. They went singly or in colonies; for a time they had to endure, but soon their endurance brought comfort and enjoyment, and, in many instances, wealth. Not all who "emigrated" succeeded in improving their condition, but the failure of many of those who did fail, could have been foretold by anyone who saw how poorly equipped they were for the venture which they undertook. These foregone conclusions of failure simply prove that *some people ought never to think of moving from their present position.* They are not equal to the demand which a "move," even to the next county, puts upon them. No great good is obtained by half men or half measures, in any sphere of life. Nor can the strongest man secure success, unless he supplement his strength and energy with the necessary accompaniments. Enough money to provide against delayed crops, or for necessary tools, as well as to pay for one's land and house, is *absolutely essential,* no less (and rather more) in Mexico than in the United States.

But in Mexico an American dollar is worth two dollars, and goes as far as two dollars of the country. Thus the American immediately doubles his capital when he arrives in Mexico — that is a great factor to consider when thinking of making a home or an investment in this country.

Another very important factor to take into account is the price of labor. Here in Mexico labor costs only about one-third of what is paid for it in the United States. In this fact the American settler or investor finds his capital at once multiplied by three. With such great advantages, it would seem beyond question that any one who, after careful investigation, makes a venture in Mexico, cannot fail of success.

A FREE SERVICE.

THE Mexican Central Railway Company is one of the greatest factors in the making of modern Mexico. Of the seven thousand miles of railroad in the republic, this company owns and operates nearly two thousand miles, reaching most of the large cities. The Central *serves, directly, a large majority of the population of the country.* The company is anxious to have the regions through which its lines pass, more fully developed. Along these lines lie thousands (we may perhaps say millions) of acres of fertile land now unproductive because unused. Until recently it was scarcely possible to say that small desirable tracts of land could be obtained, for the whole country was held in vast estates. Events have combined to make it best for large owners to divide their holdings — the laws under the new régime making the old order of things unprofitable. Accordingly the time has come when these great estates of thousands of acres must be broken up, and people of small means can get for use such portions of them as they desire. The railway company has established a bureau of information, for the purpose of bringing seller and buyer together, and thus facilitate transactions. It furnishes a *free service*, but although free, just as valuable a service to both seller and buyer as if it cost them each a large fee. The business of the railway company is transportation, not speculation. It wants more stuff to transport, and hence its desire to have the country developed along its lines. Every new home established, every new enterprise undertaken, every additional acre put under cultivation along its lines, means an *increase of business*. To awaken interest, to answer inquiries, to bring about settlement and investment, is the effort of the company, through this bureau. Its service is *free*, but it is not a work of charity. It is an *investment* of the company made in the hope and belief of good returns. It is, if you please, a loan made by one department of the company's business to another department, made in the belief that the loan will be so used that the lender will be soon repaid, not only principal and interest, but a great bonus besides, which will be perpetually increasing. Please make free use of our free service.

THREE GOOD THINGS.

THREE good things are accomplished by one satisfactory transaction, such as the bureau aims to promote.

First, the owner who sells say a part of a tract now unused or only partially cultivated, will be put in a position to make more "business" out of the land which he retains than he now makes out of the whole tract, for he will have ready capital and can improve

CITY OF CHIHUAHUA

his facilities for production. Or if he sell his whole estate he will set his capital at work elsewhere making more business.

Second, the buyer who comes in with new life and energy, and with modern appliances, will be benefited. He probably will surpass his expectations, if they are not unreasonable. His prosperity and the testimony of his happy experience bring others, and so business is increased.

Third, the railroad company, increasing its volume of business, and so its revenue, will be able to devise more liberal things for its patrons, as opportunities offer. Indeed, we may add a fourth good thing to the above list. The whole country is improved by the development of its land and the enlargement of its products, for prosperity in any part is a promoter of thrift in every part.

To accomplish so great a benefit to others, as well as to do a good thing for itself, the Mexican Central Railway Company offers its service. It believes that a very valuable work is done by this bureau of information, and is glad to note that already its service is receiving substantial proofs of public appreciation.

A TRIP OVER THE ROAD.

THE best way for the reader to locate the sections which are adapted to the various branches of trade and agriculture spoken of in this book, is to make with us a trip over the Central. It is a long one, and necessarily must be a hasty one. We will merely notice less important points and give more space to those points which offer the best opportunities to the settler or to the investor. By keeping the map constantly at hand, we shall readily locate ourselves at any given point.

SOUTHWARD ON MAIN LINE.

THE first day out from the northern terminus at Ciudad Juarez (opposite El Paso), on the Rio Grande, we spend almost entirely in the state of Chihuahua, the largest state in the republic. This region offers the best opportunities on our line for the business of stock raising. The western portion of the state is noted for its rich mines. Any one who wishes to become interested in cattle or mining enterprises will do well to stop off at Chihuahua, capital of the state, and learn what representative men from all over the state, some of whom will be found in town, have to say about those things. The city is headquarters not only of the government, but of all business carried on in a state which is larger than all New England put together. You will learn more in that town in one day about Chihuahua than you can in a week anywhere else. There are already many Americans doing business in Chihuahua.

CHIHUAHUA.

LEAVING this capital, which is 225 miles from the Rio Grande, we keep on south for another two hundred miles before we pass into the next state, Durango. Just after leaving the city of Chihuahua we shall see some fine specimens of the great institutions of the country, the hacienda — that is the name for a vast estate comprising, it may be, thousands of acres of cultivated land, great herds of cattle, mines, mills, and all kinds of property under one ownership. The road here runs directly through one hacienda for more than twenty-five miles. You will also see here specimens of the implements which are used in Mexican agriculture, and which will make you think that modern appliances ought to lessen the cost of, and greatly increase, the products of the land cultivated.

A run of thirty miles up the Rio Conchos shows us specimens of irrigating canals worth seeing, as is also the fertile valley itself.

At Santa Rosalia, near the junction of the Florida with the Conchos river, is a station worth stopping at if you have the rheumatism. Near by are the springs, famous throughout and beyond Mexico. Some enterprising American might establish a sanitarium at these springs, now very poorly equipped for visitors, even for those who do not need anything but good entertainment. The scheme for a first-class sanitarium at Santa Rosalia is well worth the attention of any one whose mind runs to hotels, hospitals or specific resorts.

Fifty miles further on, up the valley of the Rio Florida, second to none in fertility, and admirably adapted to the culture of cotton, we come to Jimenez, the shipping station for the great silver region of Parral, fifty miles west of the road. Mining men will want to look into that region, perhaps. Farming men may investigate to advantage this famous Florida valley.

At Escalon a junction is made with the Mexican Northern Road, which extends northeastward seventy-five miles, to the Sierra Mojada mines, one of the largest carbonate camps in the world. Near by is another famous spring, another chance for the hotel man, and his last chance on this line in the state of Chihuahua.

Next we come to Lerdo, in Durango, on the Nazas river. Here we are in the centre of the chief cotton country of Mexico. More cotton is raised in this Laguna district than in any other part of the republic. Here are located oil mills and soap factories, which ship their goods to all points in Mexico. From Lerdo eastward through the heart of the cotton region a branch of the Mexican Central has been constructed to San Pedro, a distance of about forty miles. The large haciendas of Sacramento, Santa Teresa and San Pedro are located on this branch. Parties who may be, or may wish to become, interested in cotton, will, of course, carefully investigate this whole section. "Cotton," says one who knows, "is foreordained to be one of the chief productions, as it is already the chief staple of manufacture in Mexico." *Now* is the time to look up this matter of cotton; and at Lerdo, where forty thousand bales or more are shipped annually, the inquirer must stop and study the subject if he desires and intends to "know all about it."

Torreon, three miles south of Lerdo, is the point of junction with the Mexican International Railroad. Here connections are made for the United States and the city of Durango, about 160 miles to the west. At Torreon are located several cotton mills, which draw their supplies from the rich Laguna country in the immediate vicinity. From Torreon, south to the city of Zacatecas the road passes through a grazing country including several well-watered districts, where corn and wheat are being successfully cultivated. There are many small streams which have an abundance of water during the rainy season, and by means of dams, perfection and extension of irrigation facilities, a much larger average might be profitably cultivated. The soil is of excellent quality, and where water can be obtained, fine crops can be raised. As this section is near the mining city of Zacatecas, its products always command good prices. The machinery at Zacatecas is generally driven by horse-power, and here an enormous amount of fodder is consumed. There are several other mining camps, including Matapil, Somtrerete, and Chalchahuites in this neighborhood, but none of them are immediately on the road.

Zacatecas, a city of fifty thousand people, capital of the state of the same name, is one of the leading silver mining camps of the world. Mining has been carried on there since 1546, and the aggregate production has reached the amount of seven hundred million dollars. The present annual output is about five million dollars. The city itself is located in a comparative desert, and therefore affords an excellent market for the products of the haciendas in its vicinity.

After passing through several ranges of hills, the road descends into the valley of Aguascalientes, noted throughout the republic for its production of corn, beans and wheat. The city of Aguascalientes, capital of the state of the same name, is almost the geographical centre of the valley. It is dependent upon agriculture and manufacturing. Several woolen factories and the largest smelting plant in the republic are here located. The name Aguascalientes means "hot waters," and is derived from the hot springs in the suburbs. These waters are used in the public baths, the bath-houses being located in the immediate vicinity of the Mexican Central station. Two of the bath-houses were built by the city for the free use of the poorer people.

At Chicalote, eight miles north of Aguascalientes, is the junction with the line which, by way of San Luis Potosi, unites the main line of the Mexican Central with the port of Tampico. Here we begin our first side-trip from the main line.

EASTWARD ON TAMPICO DIVISION.

SAN LUIS POTOSI, on the Tampico Line, 130 miles from Chicalote, and 6,118 feet above sea level, is one of the most important business centres of Mexico. At this point the Tampico Branch of the Mexican Central crosses the line of the Mexican National Railway. San Luis Potosi is a manufacturing city. In the vicinity are cotton, linen, and flour mills. A considerable industry is carried on in hand weaving. This is a distributing point for a large section of country. The subtropical regions of the Rio Verde and the Huasteca are tributary to it. An extensive smelting plant, established by American capital, is in successful operation at this point. Within the last two years the city has been greatly improved by the erection of many fine buildings, and there has been a general increase in all branches of business. Many of the owners of the great mines newly discovered in the town of Posos are residents of this city, and they have added greatly to its wealth and development.

To the eastward the Tampico Line gradually descends through a country similar to that between Aguascalientes and San Luis Potosi. Crossing the eastern range at the Pass of Villar, a rapid descent to the Gulf Coast begins. This descent is made by passing through a succession of valleys, each lower than the former, until the sea level is reached. These valleys are divided from each other by mountain ranges of varying altitudes. The road enters the Rio Verde, the first of the series of valleys near its head, and skirts its edge for a distance of about thirty miles to Las Tablas.

The Rio Verde valley is one of the favored regions of Mexico. The climate is delightful, and nearly all subtropical fruits and crops, including oranges, corn, sugar-cane, beans, bananas and sweet potatoes are raised under the most favorable conditions. Through the centre of this valley flows the Rio Verde, a stream of considerable size. On the southern edge of the valley are a number of fresh-water springs, which rank among the largest in the world. The immense volume of water from these springs is distributed by means of irrigating ditches over a large acreage of land. Most of the water, however, is not utilized. There are splendid opportunities for land investment here, as not half of the country capable of being irrigated is yet under cultivation. The municipality of Rio Verde owns the right to irrigate from the largest of these springs, called the Media Luna, and the water privilege goes with the titles to the lands originating from the municipality. There is a considerable exportation of oranges from this town, and the sugar industry is also of great importance.

From Rio Verde the road passes between low and barren hills until the station of Las Canoas is reached, at the head of the Tamasopo Cañon. At the lower end of the cañon, at the station of Zacate, the real tropical country begins. In this vicinity coffee is being successfully cultivated. This is on the eastern slope of the mountains and is a region where severe droughts are unknown, because the "northers," which are the prevailing winds in the winter, or dry season, deposit heavy dews, making irrigation unnecessary except for certain crops. Coffee, oranges, bananas, sugar-cane, manioc, limes, ginger and all other tropical fruits grow in this region.

From Zacate the road follows one of the tributaries of the Panuco, until, passing through the cañon of El Abra, it descends into the plains bordering on the gulf.

In order to avoid difficulties in engineering the line was continued to the north, avoiding the larger streams, but crossing many small rivers, until it reaches the Tamesi, five miles from Tampico.

The plains west of Tampico are perfectly adapted to the cultivation of all tropical productions. Their fertility is unlimited; transportation facilities, both by land and water, are first class; labor is abundant; land is cheap; and there is no tropical region in the world so free from the malarial complaints peculiar to southern and well-watered countries. On the bottom-lands rice can be raised, and in the foothills to the westward which rise to 3,500 feet above sea level, all the various subtropical fruits grow luxuriantly.

An important cattle industry is being carried on in this section, from which much wealth has been accumulated. The success of the stock-raising industry is largely due to the peculiar property of a grass known as " Para," which is ever green and of luxuriant growth. The cattle feeding on it have to do so little travelling to get their food, and live with so little exertion, that they are constantly fat.

The banana industry, which has proved so profitable in Guatemala and Central American countries, could be even more successfully carried on in this region. All varieties of the plant grow here, and the transportation facilities enable the producer to put his fruit on board steamers within twenty-four hours after it leaves the plantation.

Tampico, at the mouth of the Panuco river, 406 miles from the main line, is rapidly becoming the principal gulf port of the republic. This is due to the complete success of the jetties built by the Mexican Central Railway Company at the mouth of the Panuco, enabling ocean steamers to discharge at the wharf, thus abolishing lighterage charges and facilitating the careful handling of goods. More than forty ocean steamers touch monthly at this port. Regular lines are now plying between New York, Mobile, New Orleans, Pensacola, Havana, European ports, Progresso and the southern seaboard cities of the Mexican gulf.

The fisheries at Tampico are the finest on the gulf, and present admirable opportunities for the establishment of canning factories to supply the home market, which now depends on Europe and the United States. As the fish are abundant and the harbor improvements make the banks easy of access in all weathers, this industry could be carried on during the entire year, and at the present time without a competitor in the republic.

SOUTH AGAIN — MAIN LINE.

RETURNING to the Main Line: From Aguascalientes, the line runs south through rolling hills until it descends into the Lagos valley. Lagos is a manufacturing city of about thirty thousand inhabitants, and is situated in one of the most fertile regions of the great table-land of Mexico. A branch of the Lerma river runs through this valley, and its waters are largely used both for the running of mills and for irrigation. One of the principal agricultural products of this valley is chile, or red pepper, which is shipped to all parts of the republic, and is highly esteemed for its excellent flavor. Wheat, corn, beans and chickpeas of superior quality are also produced in abundance.

Leaving Lagos, the line passes through a range of hills, reaches Francisco and descends into the Bajio, the most extensive valley of the republic. This is the great wheat raising country of Mexico. The cities of Silao, Leon, and Celaya, and the towns of Irapuato, Salamanca, Valle de Santiago, Pueblos del Rincon, besides hundreds of haciendas, each having as many inhabitants as a town, are situated in this region. Leon, "Queen of the Bajio," is the largest city in the valley. It has about eighty thousand inhabitants, and, on account of the cheapness of its food products, has become an important manufacturing center. While there are but few large factories, the manufacture of cotton and woolen goods, small iron ware, rebosas, serapes, leather goods, clothes, hats, etc., is carried on in thousands of private houses. The goods are largely sold to dealers for distribution to all parts of the republic. In Leon and other cities of the Bajio, admirable opportunities are afforded foreign artisans with small capital to establish a paying business. By taking advantage of the cheap labor and improving upon the articles of native manufacture a lucrative trade could be secured. Agricultural laborers in this region earn from twenty-five to thirty-one cents per day, Mexican money; carpenters, from fifty cents to one dollar; masons, painters and other artisans about the same. The Bajio lies mostly in the state of Guanajuato, though portions of it extend into the neighboring state of Jalisco.

At Silao, twenty miles south of Leon, is the junction of the Guanajuato Branch of the Mexican Central which connects the main line with the capital of the state. Guanajuato is a mining town of about fifty thousand inhabitants. The annual production of silver at the present time is about $3,500,000. The city affords a first-class market for the agricultural products of the Bajio, on the eastern edge of which it is situated.

HERCULES COTTON MILL

WESTWARD — GUADALAJARA DIVISION.

FROM Irapuato, twenty miles south of Leon, the Guadalajara Branch of the Central runs west to Ameca. Irapuato is a town of about twenty-five thousand inhabitants, and is situated in a very fertile region especially adapted to the cultivation of small fruits and vegetables. The strawberry here ripens all the year round. The Guadalajara Branch follows the Lerma river through an extensive valley in which all the products of the temperate zone are raised. The crops here never fail from drought. The principal towns of this region are Penjamo, eight thousand inhabitants; La Piedad, about the same; La Barca, ten thousand inhabitants; Ocotlan, eight thousand inhabitants (this is the port through which the trade of Lake Chapala passes); Guadalajara, a city of ninety thousand inhabitants, and Ameca, the terminus, ten thousand inhabitants. West of Guadalajara the line descends into the sub-tropical country whose soil and climate are favorable to the production of all kinds of fruits, as well as coffee, cotton, sugar and tobacco. Ameca is situated in the beautiful Ameca valley. It is the distributing point for the Mascota, Autlan, Huachinango and other regions to the westward, and also the center of a rich mineral district. The tequila of the Guadalajara and Ameca districts is exported in large quantities to all parts of the country.

SOUTHWARD ON MAIN LINE.

RETURNING again to the Main Line: Between Irapuato and Queretaro the line passes through a country very similar to that in the vicinity of Leon and along the Guadalajara Branch. The towns of Salamanca, fifteen thousand inhabitants; Valle de Santiago, ten thousand inhabitants, which is connected with Salamanca by a tramway ten miles in length; Guaje, five thousand inhabitants, and Celaya, thirty thousand inhabitants, lie in this region.

Queretaro has a population of about fifty thousand inhabitants, and is an important manufacturing city. At this point there are several large cotton and flour mills in operation. The mills employ over two thousand hands. South of the city is the celebrated Cañada, noted for its great number of small orchards and market gardens. At the head of the Cañada is a fine spring, which has been improved by the municipality for bathing purposes. There are free baths for the poorer people. The water of the spring is also used for irrigating the gardens of the Cañada. In the vicinity of Celaya there are also a number of woolen and flour mills. Here the celebrated confectionery called "cajete" is manufactured.

Leaving the Cañada the line climbs through a low pass and gradually descends to the valley of San Juan Del Rio. This is a very fertile region, devoted principally to the cultivation of corn, beans and wheat. In the valley there are many extensive dams for irrigating purposes.

From San Juan Del Rio the line ascends to Leña, the highest point on the road, passing over a rolling country devoted to the raising of cattle. From Leña a rapid descent is made to the valley of the Tula river, a region quite similar to that in the vicinity of San Juan Del Rio. Here we see for the first time on our line the maguey plant cultivated extensively. Proximity to the city of Mexico here makes it possible to market pulque, the native drink extracted from this plant.

From Tula a branch of the Mexican Central runs to Pachuca, forty-four miles to the eastward. Pachuca is the centre of a large silver mining district. The reduction of ores is also carried on there to a large extent by the "Patio" process. Going south from Tula on the main line there is a gradual ascent until passing through the famous cut of Nochistongo the valley of Mexico is reached, and soon our journey from the border to the capital comes to an end in the city of Mexico.

Thus hastily we have made an excursion over nearly two thousand miles of railroad. We have seen in the thirteen states of Mexico which we have passed through, a great variety of vegetation; we have learned something about the country which is tributary to the Mexican Central Railway, and which that railway is endeavoring to develop. We have had only a glimpse of this wonderful land, but now we are better prepared than we were before this glimpse, to learn more in detail some facts concerning those products of Mexico which offer the greatest inducements to settlers and investors.

THE MINING INDUSTRY.

THE great mineral belt of Mexico which has produced one-third of the silver now existing in the world, extends from northwest to southeast, and lies in almost its entire extent contiguous to points on the Mexican Central Railway. For three hundred and fifty years it has been producing its millions annually, but never before as much as at the present time. New mines are constantly being discovered and old ones reopened. The production in 1896 was the greatest in the history of the country, amounting to seventy million dollars, including gold, silver, lead and copper. Recent developments at Posos, in the state of Guanajuato, and at Inde, El Oro and Guanacevi, in the state of Durango, and many newer discoveries, demonstrate the fact that in this belt the miner has almost a virgin field for prospecting. The production of the old mines at Guanajuato, Zacatecas and Pachuca has continued about the same for more than a century.

The more important new districts are the mineral regions around the town of Mazapil, east from the station Camacho, on our main line, and those near the cities of Guadalajara and Ameca on the Guadalajara Branch.

As a rule the mineral sections of Mexico are not sterile, as is so often the case in the United States and other countries. Another advantage is, that labor is cheap and abundant, and that there is absolute freedom from strikes and troubles of a kindred nature; also the fact that as this country is on a silver basis, all labor and supplies are paid for in that metal.

THE CATTLE INDUSTRY.

THE cattle industry is confined to no particular section. Where the rains are insufficient to produce corn crops, as is the case in considerable portions of Chihuahua, Durango and Coahuila, the grass in ordinary years is sufficient for grazing and even for the fattening of stock. More commonly, however, the thin stock from the northern part of the republic is fattened on the haciendas of the central and southern portions. Of late years an industry has grown up in the eastern portion of the states of San Luis Potosi, Southern Tamaulipas and Northern Vera Cruz, which, although yet in its infancy, is still very important. Taking advantage of the wonderful properties of the "Para" grass, the stockmen in this region purchase lean stock in the grazing countries of the northern and eastern part of the republic and fatten it for the Pachuca, Puebla, city of Mexico and Yucatan markets. Lean stock can be bought for from five to fifteen dollars per head, and when fattened it is worth from twenty to forty-five dollars a head. It is estimated that one acre of good ground in Para grass, if cut and fed will feed two head of stock the year round; in pasture, three acres will fatten four head. The grass is ever green, of luxuriant growth, very nourishing, and will exterminate all weeds. This low country region, though admirably adapted to the fattening of stock, is not as favorable to breeding as the higher plains of Durango and Chihuahua, because here flies and ticks bother the very young stock. But while in the higher altitudes they are able to breed a very large number of cattle, the pasturage at times, toward the end of the dry season, is so scarce that there is danger of loss from starvation if many are not shipped to other points.

AGRICULTURE ON THE TABLE-LANDS.

ON the Central Plateau both agricultural conditions and climate strongly resemble those of California; the same crops and fruits are raised. The most noticeable differences are, that first, the temperature is much more even in Mexico; and second, that the rainy season comes in summer instead of in winter. As a rule, beans and barley are raised without irrigation, while crops of wheat, alfalfa and vegetables must be irrigated. As many of the cities and mining camps are distributed over this plateau, a market is always near at hand at remunerative prices. The methods of cultivation are very primitive. The Bajio, the Lerma

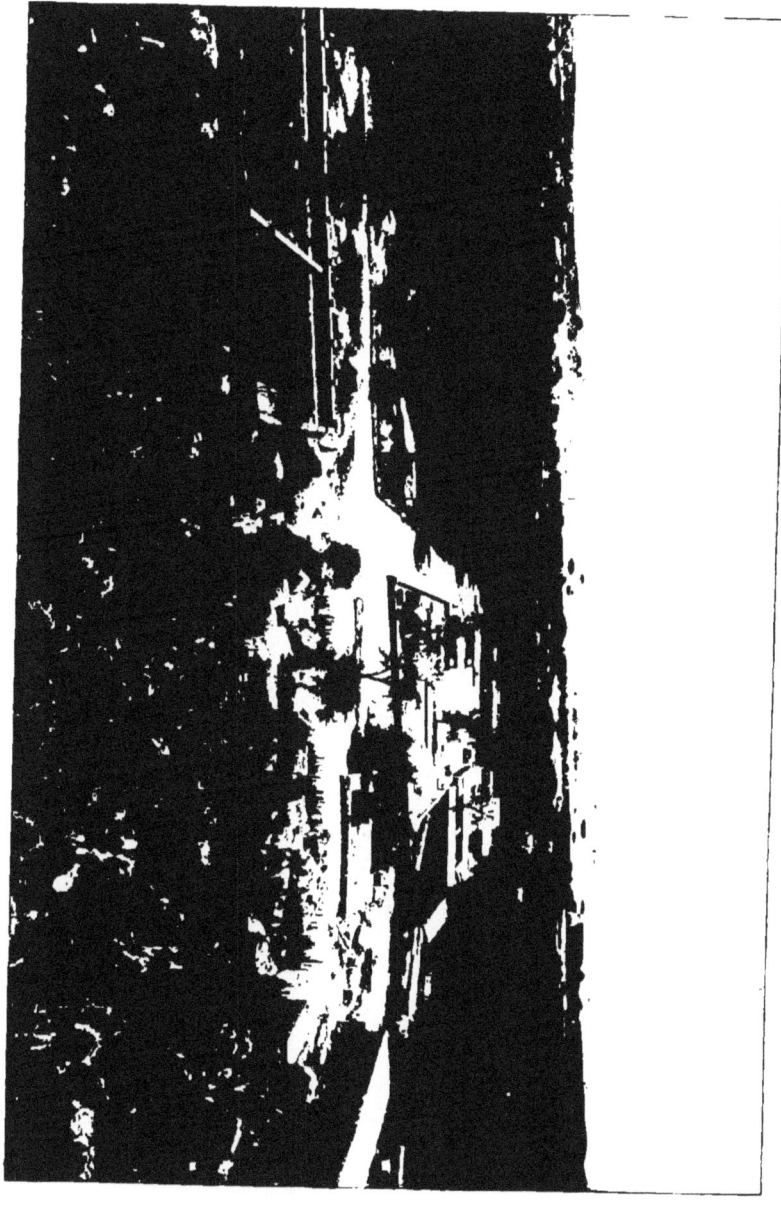

RANCH SCENE

valley, and the regions tributary to Lake Chapala are the most desirable portions of the plateau, for both climate and fertility. In these regions many haciendas are for sale at fair prices.

SUBTROPICAL AGRICULTURE.

SUBTROPICAL sections are those which lie below the frost line and above the torrid and swampy portions of the coast. In general terms, regions from two hundred to three thousand feet above the sea level which are free from heavy frost and exempt from excessive heat and drought, and which produce their various crops the year round, are subtropical regions. Vanilla, coffee, tobacco, oranges, corn, beans, ginger, manioc, sugar, lemons, citrons, pineapples, bananas, pomegranates, melons, aguacates, plums, chirimoyas, india-rubber trees, and nearly all garden products flourish in the various altitudes of these sections. Besides the products already named, many others, locally known, grow here. A perpetual succession of crops is the rule.

The health conditions here are unsurpassed. The bronchial, rheumatic and lung troubles of a colder and more variable climate are almost unknown, as are also the malarial affections of tropical sections. The valleys of the Mississippi and of the Missouri are more malarial than are these southern sidehills. Climatic conditions are more affected by the general direction of the wind than by absolute altitude. Places at sea level feeling the refreshing effects of the ocean winds, are found to be much more healthy than valleys of 3,500 and 4,000 feet elevation which are shut in by mountains.

A REMARKABLE REGION.

IN the foothills near the eastern coast, north of the range which approaches the gulf above the city of Vera Cruz, and south of Tuxpan, lies one of the most fertile and delightful regions on the face of the globe. Through it runs the Panuco river and its tributaries, giving the region cheap and convenient water transportation to the port of Tampico. It is well watered, and unlike the corresponding country on the Pacific slope, very slightly disturbed by vicissitudes of climate. Railroad communication with

Tampico by way of the station at Valles is quick, and rates, regulated by government, are low. The location and the facilities for transportation are unsurpassed in Mexico. This section is rapidly coming to the front, and is well worthy the careful investigation of any one who wishes to make a venture in Mexico. No other section in any part of the country presents so complete a combination of advantages to the investor: healthy climate, regular rainfall, plenty of reliable and cheap labor, rich land, a great variety of crops and low rates of transportation. Here sugarcane is perennial, and goes to seed. Ginger is plentiful in the mountains, as are also lemons, limes, sweet oranges and sarsaparilla. Corn and Para grass flourish here, and the guyaba grows wild in the forests. This is the famous Huasteca Potosina section. Here coffee of the finest quality grows more luxuriantly than in any other part of Mexico, and, perhaps, than in any other part of the world. Already great progress has been made here in the raising of coffee. The planting during the past three years has increased at the rate of sixty per cent each year. The town of Xilitla, forty-five miles southwest of Valles, is the headquarters for coffee producers. For several years the value of the annual exportation of coffee from this region has exceeded two million dollars.

Coffee seems to be indigenous here. Trees growing wild in the forest give very good crops. During the forty-three years in which the coffee berry has been raised here there has been but one crop failure. That certainly beats the Kansas record on corn, and demonstrates that the conditions here are all favorable to the growth of coffee. Some fabulous stories are told of production here, but we are not giving fables to our readers. The price of land in the Huasteca naturally is higher than in less favored parts of Mexico, but the land is worth more, estimated by its returns. The *best* lands are cheapest in the long run everywhere. Land already in coffee costs about one hundred dollars an acre, but equally good land (now covered with jungle) adapted to the growth of coffee and other products can be bought in small tracts for about eight dollars per hectave ($2\tfrac{4}{10}$

acres), or say four dollars per acre. An acre of land will accommodate between four hundred and six hundred coffee trees.

A writer in the St. Louis *Globe-Democrat* (Nov. 28, 1896,) calls the Xilitla district (pronounced He-leet-la) "a Mexican paradise," and tells what makes it so. He says: "It is a strip of mountain side thirty miles long, and from twelve to fifteen miles wide. It is like a canoe resting on its side. There are mountains behind, mountains on the south and mountains on the north. To the east is the Gulf of Mexico, a hundred miles away. The moist, warm clouds form on the gulf, drift westward across the coast country, and are pocketed in this scooped-out section of the mountain range. They encounter the colder currents and precipitate their moisture. Thus Xilitla gets its almost weekly rain. The addition of the hot sun makes it a Mexican paradise. Such stories as are told of vegetation are beyond evidence until the proof of them is seen. Here a pineapple plant set out in March will produce in the next December, and, once started, it will keep on producing. The same is true of sugar-cane and of bananas. Once planted they are planted for good. Two years ago Dr. Whitfield, a Mississippian, who owns a plantation in this wonderful section, received from Florida an orange slip eight inches long. After eighteen months' growth it had upon it eighty-four oranges. He adds: "The glory of Xilitla's fertility is the coffee tree. In China the rule is 1,100 trees to the acre, but in this section, so much more luxuriant is the growth, the limit is only 450 trees to the acre."

Speaking of the "labor" of this mountain paradise, he says: "The native population is the Huastecos. These Indians are the remnant of a once numerous tribe. They are clean, honest and industrious. No doors are locked in Xilitla. Coffee planters go away and leave guns and all manner of personal property in their houses, but lose nothing. When it is said that the Huastecos are industrious, the Huastecan standard of industry must be borne in mind. Four days here make a week of labor. The Indian does that four days' work for one dollar. If he were paid two or four dollars he would work only four days. The dollar is paid in advance — on Sunday. Payment insures the delivery of the four days' work before Saturday night. If the work is not done, the Indian is a defaulter in the light of the local laws. On Sunday Xilitla has a population of five thousand, but on Monday not two hundred Indians are to be found in town. The others are out on the plantations.

" Coffee growing," says this observant and cautious writer, " is profitable in Xilitla, but it doesn't give the magnificent returns which people in the States read about in the prospectuses of Mexican companies having coffee lands to sell. If the labor were not cheap beyond comparison, the profits would be only moderate. The yield of coffee trees is about one-fourth of what is claimed to tempt investors. The planter almost always overestimates his crop; he will point to trees which he will claim have eight pounds on them, but the harvest will show not more than two or three pounds to these same trees. In a plantation with four hundred to six hundred trees to the acre, two and a half pounds to the tree is a good average crop."

Outside of this Xilitla district, so peculiarly adapted to coffee, there lies an extensive region in this Huasteca country, where fine opportunities are presented for the production of a great variety of crops, such as oranges, pineapples, vanilla, ginger, sugar, corn, bananas, tobacco and india-rubber trees. Perhaps in view of the limited supply of india rubber now in sight anywhere in the world and of the constantly increasing demand for it, its cultivation offers greater inducement to capital than the raising of anything else that grows. This section is worthy the attention of any one having in mind this enterprise.

Says Mr. Lummis, "Rubber, which becomes more important every year, as we need more and find less, is an industry barely born in Mexico. There are but two plantations of over five thousand trees, yet millions of acres in the republic are as perfectly adapted to caout-chouc (koo-chook) culture as the most favored spots in the Amazonas of Peru." Among the "millions of acres" referred to by Mr. Lummis, many will be found in this remarkable region west of Tampico.

A COFFEE GROVE

COFFEE.

IN the previous pages upon the Huasteca region something has been said upon coffee, its principal product. A little more in detail. Now we may remark that coffee culture is one of the few industries which can be successfully pursued by the poor man, the man of moderate means and the millionaire. Within the last few years a great deal of truth, and much which borders on fiction, has been said and written on coffee raising. •There is, perhaps, no other investment which, when properly taken care of, will give more satisfactory returns, and which is, at the same time, non-speculative in its nature.

The soil and climatic conditions necessary to the successful production of this berry, on a commercial scale, are so peculiar that, though it grows more or less in all countries situated within the tropics, the acreage well adapted to its culture is comparatively small. Entire absence of extremes of heat and cold, a moist atmosphere, a fertile soil and absence from droughts are indispensable to the production of remunerative crops. On fertile land, in regions of the climatic conditions mentioned, the energetic man with moderate capital can be sure of returns rarely realized from other industries on a like investment. The books published on this subject give a great variety of facts and figures; but in general terms it costs in Mexico seven dollars, silver, per hundred pounds to raise, pick, clean and sack coffee. The selling price at the plantation has ranged at about twenty-seven dollars per hundred pounds for the past three years. The production per acre runs from two hundred and fifty to five hundred pounds. These results are obtained from ordinary cultivation, but they can be greatly augmented by improved methods, as no plant more readily responds to high cultivation than the coffee tree.

Taking into consideration the fact that the coffee planter lives in one of the most delightful climates on the face of the earth, and that besides his main crop he may raise oranges, bananas and all subtropical fruits, together with most of the vegetables found in northern gardens, conditions are certainly most favorable.

After the plantation is well organized and on a paying basis, it is only necessary for the owner to be on it during the picking season, which comes in the delightful months of winter. In fact, it is perfectly feasible for a man to run a fruit farm in the North and a coffee farm in Mexico at the same time. If the winter season, which is a dead loss to so many of our northern agriculturists, could be used by them in coffee production, it would prove a great help to their income, and afford them a delightful way to pass the winter.

BANANAS.

THE increased consumption of tropical fruits in northern countries within the last two decades is one of the remarkable results consequent of our improved transportation facilities. The ports of New York, Philadelphia, New Orleans, Boston, Baltimore and Mobile receive these fruits by the steamer load, and distribute them to the thousands of interior cities and villages of the United States. Short lines of railroads have been built here in Mexico to take bananas and oranges to the coast, and swift steamer lines established to carry them north, yet the markets are never flooded.

Baron Humbolt says that "an acre of ground planted in bananas will produce more food at a less cost than any other known crop." Another authority has declared that "the banana is the most productive of all the fruits of the world. It produces forty-four times as much as the potato and one hundred and thirty-one times as much as wheat." These statements appear to be exaggerations, but they are merely expressions of actual facts. The greatest market in the world for these products is the United States, where are the greatest number of well-to-do people who have money to spend, and spend it for these luxuries. Yet the field best adapted to the cultivation of the banana, and at the same time the field nearest to the United States, is neglected. We refer to the hill country tributary to the port of Tampico. Here thrives every variety of tropical fruits. Oranges, bananas, pineapples, guavas, chicas, lemons and granaditas grow here to perfection. Frequent rains, fertile soil, heavy dews, rolling hills, which promote drainage and help irrigation, cheap lands, cheap labor and first-class transportation facilities (either by rail or water), contribute to make the raising and marketing of these products profitable. This is one of the few places within the tropics where the Anglo-Saxon can live and be healthy while he cultivates the soil; and yet the principal exportation of bananas is from points more distant from the United States than Mexico, and where labor is paid in gold.

An acre of land will produce annually from seven hundred to eight hundred bunches of bananas at a cost of not over eight cents a bunch. These are worth at the plantation forty cents a bunch, and yield a net profit of $225 or more per acre, Mexican money.

The capital necessary to establish such a plantation is much less than in the case of coffee, sugar or oranges. The plants come into bearing within ten months after being planted, and are not affected by blight or other diseases.

Between the West Indian, Central American and United States ports more than thirty steamers are engaged in this trade. The port of New Orleans alone receives something like seven million bunches of bananas annually. The yearly importation of the United States is in the neighborhood of sixteen million dollars, gold. This sum, representing about thirty million dollars, Mexican money, should, and in the near future will, largely come to Mexico. When the many advantages offered by our fertile soil, cheap labor and land, and absolute freedom from internal disorders, are appreciated by the capitalist and fruit grower, the many investments will be made here. The local market is of considerable importance, and it is increasing.

Eight thousand dollars, Mexican money, is estimated to be sufficient to purchase, clear, build ditches, plant and cultivate seventy acres of land for the first two years. During that period the plantation will yield fifty-four thousand bunches of bananas, worth at least forty cents a bunch at the plantation. Not less than fifty thousand bunches will be produced annually thereafter, at a cost of from six to eight cents a bunch for cultivation and harvesting.

The cultivation of the banana is very simple, and there is probably no fruit which gives as quick returns. Nine months after the suckers are set out the fruit is ready for cutting, and thereafter three and even four crops a year can be obtained. A rich virgin soil, such as that of the region mentioned, may be cropped for many years without requiring the use of fertilizers, and, when irrigated, will produce indefinitely. There are many varieties of bananas cultivated in tropical America, varying from the size of the musk-flavored specimens, smaller than one's little finger (known in Mexico as "Ciento en boca") to others nearly a foot in length.

The by-products of the banana are numerous. The fruit can be dried and preserved, like figs, or reduced to a sugary powder. It also yields, by distillation, a kind of brandy; the stem and leaves of the plant are used in the manufacture of paper. The plantain, a species of banana, yields a fruit much larger than the banana, but too coarse to be eaten raw. This fruit, however, is eaten when boiled, roasted or fried like a vegetable, and is highly prized by the inhabitants of the southern countries. From another variety, the manilla plantain (Musa textilis), the fibre known as "manilla hemp" is obtained. This plant could also be cultivated in Mexico, the conditions of soil and climate being the same as in the Philippine Islands, where it is indigenous.

SUGAR.

THE production of sugar in Mexico is carried on both by the wealthy planter, with his hundreds of thousands of dollars invested in lands and refineries, and by the poor renter with his few acres of ground, his wooden rolls and copper kettle. The rich man produces the refined white sugar, and the poor man produces the various classes of brown sugar, known in Mexico as "Piloncillo," "Panocha" and "Panela," which, when fresh, resemble maple-sugar. In regions well adapted to cane raising, the money value per acre of the annual production is probably

CANOAS VALLEY ON TAMPICO DIVISION

greater than that of any other crop, with the possible exception of the coffee or orange. The sugar industry may be begun on a small scale with a limited capital, and may be developed to any extent. A few more acres can be cultivated each year, another "Trapiche" put in, and a kettle or two added to the plant, until the production warrants an investment in refining machinery for the production of the white article. In fact, the most successful and best paying plantations have been built up in this way. Sugar, in the region adapted to its cultivation, is one of the most certain crops, as it has no enemy except frost.

The irrigated portion of the Rio Verde valley, east from San Bartolo on our Tampico Line, the foothill country westward of Tampico, and the river bottoms of the Ameca valley in Western Jalisco, tributary to our Guadalajara Branch, contain much fine sugar land. These tracts all have the advantage of being near lines of transportation, a factor which is indispensable to successful production of sugar in this country.

CLIMATE.

ALL the various climates of Mexico resemble each other in certain particulars. We have no sudden changes, no extremes of heat and cold, no heavy, prolonged storms. There is but a small difference in temperature between summer and winter. The great Interior Plateau, which varies in altitude from three thousand five hundred feet, in the north, to seven thousand feet, in the south, has an exceedingly dry climate, and is almost absolutely free from malaria. This plateau presents at many points, conditions which are especially favorable to those afflicted with bronchial, rheumatic or pulmonary troubles. The coast valleys, at an altitude of from five hundred to three thousand feet, have a climate resembling perpetual spring. They are green at all seasons of the year, and are so sheltered among the mountains that neither heat nor cold need be guarded against. Only the swampy regions near the coast are malarial, and even these are far less malarial than they are commonly supposed to be. The following climatic table of government observations shows the even temperature of the principal cities of the Mexican republic.

CLIMATIC TABLES OF REPUBLIC OF MEXICO.

FURNISHED BY PROF. M. BARCENA, DIRECTOR OF THE GOVERNMENT OBSERVATORY, CHAPULTEPEC, CITY OF MEXICO.

Showing the Average Monthly Temperature (Fahrenheit) at Various Cities on the Lines of the Mexican Central Railway, year ending Dec. 31, 1894.

LOCATION.	JANUARY.	FEBRUARY.	MARCH.	APRIL.	MAY.	JUNE.	JULY.	AUGUST.	SEPTEMBER.	OCTOBER.	NOVEMBER.	DECEMBER.	Elevation Above Sea Level.
Mexico	53.8°	56.7°	60.4°	64.0°	64.6°	63.7°	62.4°	61.9°	62.1°	58.5°	55.6°	53.4°	7,349 feet
San Juan del Rio	59.2	61.5	65.5	70.5	71.2	70.5	66.9	67.5	65.7	64.8	58.5	56.8	6,245 "
Queretaro	60.1	61.5	65.3	71.1	72.3	70.9	67.5	68.9	64.2	63.0	59.5	56.7	5,904 "
Silao	59.2	61.2	63.3	70.2	74.7	74.3	69.4	69.6	68.9	64.8	59.7	57.7	5,828 "
Guanajuato	56.8	62.4	61.7	69.3	71.1	71.1	68.2	66.0	63.3	62.2	62.1	57.9	6,837 "
Leon	58.3	61.2	63.1	70.9	74.3	74.8	68.7	68.9	67.6	63.7	58.3	56.8	5,863 "
Aguascalientes	55.0	61.2	60.3	68.5	73.9	74.4	71.4	69.4	68.9	64.0	61.5	55.9	6,179 "
San Luis Potosi	57.0	59.7	63.3	68.9	71.8	71.6	68.2	68.5	67.8	62.2	56.8	54.3	6,118 "
Pachuca	54.5	58.6	60.1	61.3	61.0	61.9	66.9	61.3	62.2	59.5	53.2	54.1	7,831 "
Zacatecas	54.5	56.1	58.6	66.0	70.0	68.4	62.1	62.8	62.2	60.6	55.4	55.6	8,044 "
Guadalajara	59.5	62.6	69.8	70.9	73.6	73.6	73.4	69.8	69.8	66.4	62.8	60.4	5,054 "
Lagos	60.6	61.0	62.4	63.9	69.3	68.7	69.8	68.7	66.9	64.2	60.6	59.4	6,134 "
Tampico	.....	.....	.....	75.0	77.7	82.4	81.1	81.5	80.1	77.4	69.1	71.2	Sea Level, Gulf Port.

It is justly claimed that Mexico is the best of summer resorts. Does not the above showing warrant this assertion?

Average summer temperature in the city of Mexico during the past fifteen years, 63° Fahrenheit in the shade.

MANUFACTURING.

WHILE the conditions in Mexico at present, perhaps, are not favorable to the establishment of large manufacturing centres, such as are found in the United States and Europe, where millions of capital and thousands of employees are under the direction of one corporation, the small manufacturer will here find a very encouraging outlook. The manufacturer who in person directs his employees, and who depends to a large extent on his own skill, energy and business talent for success in any enterprise, need seek no further for a field in which to employ his knowledge and ability. Mexico is to-day unequalled in the world (except, perhaps, by Japan) as a field for the small manufacturer, who finds himself, in the United States and Europe, crowded out of the market by the tyranny of trusts and of organized labor.

The docility, skill and imitative faculties of the native artisan make him a desirable employee. The cheapness of food products and the mildness of the climate both conduce to production of goods at an exceedingly small cost.

Where the temperate and torrid zones shade into each other, and where pine, mahogany, bamboo, cotton, wool and hides are produced in great profusion within a distance of but one day's travel, transportation of raw products is not a large item in the cost of the finished article. The laborer can afford to work for low wages, as he loses no time by heat or cold, has no long winter to provide for, and has no fear of scarcity of food products. The abundance of water power, the sentiment of the government (both general and local) in favor of establishing and fostering home enterprises, the fact that within her borders almost every substance necessary to man is produced, and the silver basis of the country affording cheap labor, all combine to make the situation favorable to success. A high tariff, in connection with freight rates and exchange, gives such protection to home industries here as is found in no other country in the world.

The home market is increasing by bounds and strides. Of the thirteen million inhabitants of the republic, only a small portion, until lately, has had the means to purchase many things which in other countries are considered necessities, but which, heretofore, were considered luxuries in Mexico. The extended educational system; the great prosperity throughout the republic resulting from railroad extension, and from the large amount of money which it has put into circulation; the example of foreign colonists, who are increasing every year; the growth in population which has followed upon peace and security; all these have led to a much larger demand for all kinds of goods among the middle and lower classes than there was in former years.

Mexico, for the manufacturer, has many inviting prospects. The cotton and woolen industries, which are growing at such a rapid rate, show what can be done in other branches. Shoes, crockery, glass and small iron ware, tools, sewing-machines, hats, clothing, and the thousand and one articles which are the necessities of civilized life, could and should all be manufactured at home. The conditions are such as to favor successful competition with articles now imported, and also exportation of such products to other countries.

Another point to be taken into consideration is, that in Mexico the local conditions are such that industries are not controlled by monopolies and trusts, which, by preventing honest competition, maintain artificially high prices, and, at the same time, crush poorer competitors and reduce the wages of employees. The geographical and climatic conditions of the republic, as well as the social ones, are not favorable to those monopolies which have been so fatal to the interests of other countries. In Mexico the local manufacturer supplies the local wants, and whoever first establishes a plant for the supply of any particular district, with some staple manufactured article, will receive an abundant reward. The conditions are particularly favorable to the small manufacturer who can invest ten, twenty or fifty thousand dollars in a factory with the latest and best appliances, and compete with any imported article in quality and price.

HEALTH CONDITIONS.

THE practice of the enlightened physician is yearly tending more and more to the abandonment of drugs and to a greater reliance on diet, climate and the use of those remedies provided by nature in thermal springs. The resorts of Europe are annually visited by thousands of ailing Americans, who, in their search for health, leave behind them millions of dollars. Conditions in Mexico are especially favorable for the organization of similar establishments, which, under competent management, either on a large or small scale, cannot fail to prove remunerative.

All varieties of both hot and cold water springs are to be found in this republic in the immediate vicinity of lines of travel, and at altitudes varying from sea level to nine thousand feet above it. We have every variety of mild climate, from the perpetual spring of the foothills to the dry and bracing air of the central plains.

These several climates are so exempt from sudden changes, that the most delicate invalid is not subject to the shocks from heat and cold which are experienced in other latitudes. The opportunities for providing a varied and palatable diet to tempt the uncertain appetite of the invalid are all that can be desired. Fresh fruits and vegetables are in season during the entire year. The picturesqueness of the country, the strange social life of the natives, and the abundance of game, afford amusement and occupation while nature is working her cure. Another advantage that will contribute to the success of these establishments in Mexico is that they may be kept open throughout the year; they need never be closed. The summer months are cool, the winter months are warm, and the capitalist establishing a resort here will not be forced to make in a short season the profits to pay interest on his investment for the entire year, as he has to do in the North.

Because of the silver basis of the country, the guests will also be able, by a small expenditure, to receive the same comforts offered in similar establishments in the United States and Europe. The expenses here will be practically the same amount in silver that they are in gold in other countries. Another point: there is no ocean to be crossed to reach the health resorts of Mexico; no seasickness to be feared.

A beginning has been made already in a small way and it serves to show the possibilities in this line. Santa Rosalia, Aguascalientes, Comañilla, Ajacuha, Cuitzeo and Taninul are already visited by many in search of health, and although the accommodations are far from being on a par with those of the great resorts of Europe and the United States, the results to health are equal, if not more favorable, than those obtained in more pretentious establishments.

Rheumatic, bronchial and pulmonary troubles can nowhere be more quickly cured than in the light, dry and bracing air of the Mexican uplands, aided by the healing effects of the thermal springs.

The tired nerves and exhausted brain of the overworked man of affairs can find in the ever green foothills of the coast, that rest so necessary to his recuperation. There quaint and ancient Indian villages, strange animals and stranger vegetation compel him to forget for a season the struggle for wealth.

A MISTAKE CORRECTED.

ONE of the most erroneous opinions that has gained currency in northern countries, is that health is more precarious and disease more virulent in southern latitudes than in the North. Many causes have contributed to establish this belief. Each region has its own peculiar ailments. We become accustomed to sickness that we see around us every day, while an unknown disease with an unfamiliar name causes a dread not felt for what we are familiar with.

A warm climate, while an absolute preventive of one form of disease, induces the habits of living (especially among the lower classes) favorable to another. Foreigners in Mexico who conform to the conditions of the country are as healthy as they would be at home.

Centenarians are not rarer in the South than in the North. A subtropical climate conduces to long life, an active brain and quiet nerves. It is not detrimental to either physical or mental development, but it does prevent to a great extent, that extreme nervous energy so common in the North, which in many cases results in heart failure or nervous prostration.

ORANGE CULTURE IN MEXICO.

THE wonderful growth of the orange export trade from Mexico to the United States, and the interest now manifested by American growers in the Mexican orange industry, prompt the following remarks concerning orange lands and orange culture along the line of the Mexican Central Railway. We speak chiefly of two sections of country: One is the foothill country just west of the port of Tampico. The other section is along the Guadalajara Branch, in the state of Jalisco.

Undeveloped land adapted to orange culture can be bought for from three to fifteen Mexican dollars per acre, according to the quality of the land and the distance from lines of transportation. All the expenses of a plantation are paid in the Mexican dollar, which will hire more labor and go farther towards developing and maintaining a grove than American dollars will go in the United States. Remember that a gold price is paid for the product on its exportation.

Special orange train service has been inaugurated by the Mexican Central Railway between points on the Guadalajara Branch. The Mexican grower is also placed on an equality with the American grower in the matter of freight rates.

The orange season in Mexico comes between the season of Florida and that of California.

Orange trees in Mexico have been known to produce as many as ten thousand oranges, in exceptional cases. The average yield is from eight hundred to one thousand oranges. A properly cultivated and prudently managed grove at the end of five years should prove more profitable than a coffee plantation of five years' growth. The production of the orange tree increases up to the tenth or twelfth year.

The orange tree thrives best in a climate where irrigation is needed during a part of the year, for thus it is less subject to diseases of a fungoid nature and less liable to attacks from insects. Irrigated orange trees planted in good ground and well taken care of have an almost indefinite lease on life.

Prices for the fruit in regions convenient to lines of transportation, range from $6.50 to $11 per thousand on the tree. It is the usual practice of the Mexican grower to sell the fruit on the tree, the buyer picking and packing the oranges at his own expense.

At one hundred trees to the acre, with a production of eight hundred oranges to the tree, and a price of $6.50 per thousand, the yield of an acre would amount to $520. At the larger estimate and price mentioned (sometimes realized) one thousand oranges per tree at eleven dollars per thousand, the yield would amount to $1100 per acre. Large profits can be relied upon from a grove in successful bearing and near transportation lines. The Mexican orange is unsurpassed in flavor and in productiveness.

A writer in the St. Louis *Globe-Democrat* gives us a glimpse of the orange section tributary to the Guadalajara Branch, and of the profits in orange culture.

At another station the siding is full of Sante Fe fruit cars waiting to convey the orange crop to St. Louis and Chicago. The orange groves are about twenty miles north of the station. The fruit is brought in on the backs of burros. One estimate placed on the year's shipments from these groves is that they will reach three hundred cars. The harvest is just now at its height. The oranges are not large, for the growers have only just awakened to the market opportunities afforded in the United States, and have not had time to improve the quality by budding the trees. The flavor, however, is delicious. These oranges sell at three for a Mexican cent at the train. That would be six for a cent in the United States. The profit on the carload is something princely. Last season these oranges were put down in Chicago at a cost of about half a cent each. This year buyers have been through the district taking all they could get. In some instances contracts have been made not only for this, but for next year's crop. The groves are given so little care that the fruit, delicious as it is, can be said to be produced almost in a wild state. A few such years as the present and last will prompt the planting of orange orchards on a large scale in this part of Mexico.

The silver question enters into the orange growing industry. Last year Mexico sent four hundred carloads of oranges to the United States. This year, according to Consul General Crittenden's estimate, the shipments will reach six hundred carloads. Other estimates reach twelve hundred cars. With free silver labor and a gold market there is much money in Mexican orange groves. The industry feels the inspiration. New groves are being planted. Old ones are being put in condition for increased production. Orange groves live fifteen years in Mexico. The average crop is one thousand oranges to the tree. A Mexican dollar a box is the price which satisfies the grower of this

BURNING POTTERY

country very well. That means about fifty cents a box in American money. A box will hold about one hundred oranges.

THE POTTERY INDUSTRY.

CLAY in great variety and of good quality is found in large quantities near many of the important towns and cities on the line of the Mexican Central Railway. Establishments for the manufacture of brick, pottery, tiling and sewer pipe can hardly fail to prove profitable to their owners.

Native ingenuity in working clay has secured for Aguascalientes, Encarnacion and Guadalajara wares an enviable reputation among tourists. These wares are also generally used throughout the republic. This fact serves to indicate what might be accomplished by combining native skill with capital and scientific knowledge of this business.

There is no pottery plant of any importance in the republic. The home consumption of pottery is now considerable, but the greater part of even the cheaper grades is imported, and therefore very expensive.

Freight and ocean rates, breakage and duties, all combine to constitute a high protective tariff on pottery, and would seem to insure great profits to the home producer.

The natural imitative ability of the native workers in clay, the cheapness of labor and the abundance of raw material, combine to offer exceptional inducements to foreign potters to establish plants in Mexico.

THE LEATHER INDUSTRY.

CONSPICUOUS among the undeveloped industries of Mexico, the profitableness of which is assured, is the manufacture of leather.

No other country is equipped as this is by nature with those things which are essential to the production of a good quality of leather; and yet there is at the present time a large annual exportation of hides from Mexico to the United States and to Europe.

Canaigre and cascalote, two of the most valuable substances

used in tanning, are here indigenous and are produced in great abundance. On account of certain difficulties in its preparation, canaigre is not much used by the Mexican tanners. As a rule they employ cascalote and various barks. Canaigre is preferable, however, and when properly prepared performs its functions in a much shorter time than is required by cascalote.

Large quantities of canaigre are now exported from Texas and South America to Europe, in spite of the fact that the plant grows wild in Mexico and attains a high degree of perfection on the arid plains of the great central plateau. Cascalote is found in great quantities in the states of Jalisco and San Luis Potosi. It has a remarkable growth in the Rio Verde district and also in the country west of the city of Guadalajara. From the pod and the bean of cascalote tannic acid is obtained.

Mexico now exports nearly all her hides to Europe and the United States, and from these countries imports all the better grades of leather used in the republic. The hides are sold and the finished product is bought, and thus the cost of much of the leather used in Mexico is increased by jobbers' profits, by duties, and by expenses for transportation. Much of this high-class leather, if not all of it, can be manufactured here as well as in Europe, and certainly much cheaper. A well equipped tannery in Mexico could hardly fail to be very profitable. The home producer would add to his profits the larger part of the extra expenses above mentioned, and still be able to undersell the foreign article. He would also have the advantage of cheap labor, paid for in silver, while the manufacturer in other countries is obliged to employ high-priced labor, paid for in gold.

Those who are now engaged in tanning in Mexico, as a rule, produce only an inferior quality of leather, because their limited capital compels them to hurry the hides through the tanning process.

CANAIGRE.

CANAIGRE is a species of dock, the root of which yields a valuable tannic acid. It is extensively cultivated in some parts of the United States, particularly in Texas. Strange to relate, in Mexico, where it grows wild, it is an almost neglected crop. It is found in parts of the states of Durango, Coahuila, Zacatecas and Aguascalientes, where it grows on sandy plains, on hill-tops, in mountain gulches and wherever sandy soil is found.

Canaigre differs from all other substances used in tanning. It has enough good properties which other agents do not possess to justify a belief that in the future it will be used almost exclusively in the manufacture of certain grades of leather. It is an excellent substitute for gambier, and a modifier of other tannages. However, tanners are conservative, and the use of canaigre is extending more slowly than its merits warrant.

As a crop for irrigated lands, canaigre has advantages which make it very valuable in the economy of agriculture, not only on account of the considerable profits which it will yield, but because with a limited water and labor supply the tillable acreage can be almost doubled. It should be planted early in the autumn or winter months and watered until March. Probably six inches of water will make a full crop, but this depends somewhat upon climatic conditions. An excess of water is more damaging to canaigre than drought is.

It can be harvested at any season of the year, although the roots are doubtless richest in tannin just before the new growth begins. Both planting and harvesting can be done by horse-power. Machinery for its cultivation can be obtained with but small cost. Canaigre is not subject to any kind of insect pest. The profit per acre, taking into consideration the certainty of the crop and of its market, and the low cost of production, is greater than that realized on almost any other field product.

Land suitable for its cultivation costs, per acre, $2.50 and upwards, Mexican money. Living expenses, where canaigre thrives, are low because there are no cold winters to provide for. Mexico being on a silver basis, the investor who makes a venture there practically doubles his capital at once, and his living costs him only as many Mexican dollars as it would American dollars in the United States.

POLITICAL DIVISIONS OF MEXICO.

(Twenty-seven States. A Federal District. Two Territories.)

State and Abbreviation.	Pop. of State.	Capital.	Pop. of Capital.
*Aguascalientes (Ag.)	142,000	Aguascalientes	31,619
Campeche (Cam.)	99,458	Campeche	16,631
*Coahuila (Coa.)	235,638	Saltillo	19,654
Colima (Col.)	70,000	Colima	19,305
Chiapas (Chia.)	309,000	Tuxtla Gutierrez	7,882
*Chihuahua (Chih)	298,000	Chihuahua	40,000
*Durango (Du.)	287,622	Durango	42,165
*Guanajuato (Gua.)	1,047,238	Guanajuato	90,000
Guerrero (Gue.)	417,621	Chilpancingo	6,204
*Hidalgo (Hi.)	548,039	Pachuca	52,186
*Jalisco (Ja.)	1,101,863	Guadalajara	125,000
*Mexico (Me.)	838,737	Toluca	23,648
Michoacan (Mi.)	889,795	Morelia	32,287
Morelos (Mo.)	159,800	Cuernavaca	8,504
Nuevo Leon (N. L.)	309,607	Monterey	56,855
Oaxaca (Oa.)	882,539	Oaxaca	32,641
Puebla (Pu.)	979,723	Puebla	91,917
*Queretaro (Que.)	227,233	Queretaro	50,000
*San Luis Potosi (S L.)	570,814	San Luis Potosi	80,000
Sinaloa (Si.)	256,414	Culiacan	14,205
Sonora (So.)	186,823	Hermosillo	8,376
Tabasco (Tab.)	134,794	San Juan Bautista	27,036
*Tamaulipas (Tam.)	204,205	Ciudad Victoria	14,575
Tlaxcala (Tl.)	166,803	Tlaxcala	2,874
Vera Cruz (Ve.)	855,975	Xalapa	18,173
Yucatan (Yu.)	320,000	Merida	36,720
*Zacatecas (Za.)	517,000	Zacatecas	70,000
*Distrito Federal (D. F.)	484,608	Mexico	400,000
Territorio de Tepic (Te.)	144,308	Tepic	7,452
Lower California (B. C.):			
Distrito Norte	7,452	Ensenada de Todos Santos,	3,737
Distrito Sur	34,835	La Paz	16,226

*The Mexican Central Railway passes through some portion of those divisions marked by an asterisk. It will be seen from these figures that this road serves directly a very large proportion of the entire population of the republic.

THE GOVERNMENT OF MEXICO.

THE form of government in Mexico is a Federal Republic. The Constitution is very similar to that of the United States. The Constitutions of the several states also closely resemble those of the American States. Perhaps the most marked difference is that in all districts (or, as they are called in Mexico, "Partidos") there is an officer representing the person of the Governor, sometimes called Jefe Politico, sometimes Prefecto. This man is an executive officer holding a position combining some of the functions of a mayor with those of a chief of police in an American city. The President of a Board of Common Council (or, as it is called in Mexico, an "Ayuntamiento,") together with the Jefe Politico, have the functions of a mayor in an American city.

The courts are organized on the American plan, although the law is more the Roman than the English Common law. Justice is administered impartially. There is perfect religious liberty.

In 1877 General Porfirio Diaz was first elected President. At that time the country was in great disorder, on account of the French intervention and the revolutions immediately succeeding it. President Diaz has ruled with a strong hand, meting out justice to all revolutionists and bandits. The result of this policy is now, and for many years has been, patent to all residents of the republic. In no portion of the world is life or property more safe than it is in the republic of Mexico. Evil doers know that they have to deal with energetic officers. General Gonzales was President from 1880 to 1884, when General Diaz was again elected, and has since been President, having been re-elected in 1888, 1892 and 1896.

We wish to *emphasize the fact that a new era has dawned upon Mexico, and that the government, federal, state, and municipal, in this country is vigorously and impartially administered.* There was a time when things were about as bad as they could be, but under the reform administration of General Diaz abuses have been so far corrected, corruption so exposed and punished, that now throughout the country the personal rights of citizens and of foreigners are as well protected as they are in the United States. Many Americans are already living in Mexico, and few, if any of them, have had occasion since the first election of Diaz (1877) to complain of any ill usage by the government. The universal testimony of foreigners is that now Mexico is as well governed as any country in the world.

MATERIAL PROGRESS.

THE best proof of the solid industrial advancement of the Mexican republic appears in the following figures which show the steady increase in the revenues of the Federal Government during the last ten years. The increase in the revenues of the Mexican Central Railway during the same period is also striking evidence of our commercial growth and an indication of future prosperity.

What makes this showing more remarkable is the fact that within the period for which returns are given, financial panics have occurred in other countries and we have had four years of drought in this country. Mexico is on the eve of a period of material prosperity such as has been seen in no country in modern times, and investments made within her borders now are sure to bring returns which cannot fail to be most satisfactory.

RECEIPTS OF THE MEXICAN TREASURY FROM JULY 1, 1881, TO JUNE 30, 1896.

Years.	Receipts.
1881 to 1882	$30,466,093.74
1882 " 1883	32,850,931.25
1883 " 1884	37,621,065.29
1884 " 1885	30,660,434.24
1885 " 1886	28,980,895.76
1886 " 1887	32,126,509.07
1887 " 1888	40,962,045.23
1888 " 1889	34,374,783.32
1889 " 1890	38,566,601.69
1890 " 1891	37,391,804.99
1891 " 1892	37,474,879.20
1892 " 1893	42,813,455.71
1893 " 1894	40,211,747.13
1894 " 1895	43,945,699.00
1895 " 1896	50,521,407.00

VALUE OF EXPORTS.

Articles.	1895 Value.	1896 Value.
Hides,	$2,350,262	$2,403,099
Tobacco,	1,460,133	1,461,090
Fruit,	125,460	246,150
Henequén,	6,768,007	7,723,092
Chicle,	679,367	1,527,838
Copper,	2,148,184	3,909,485
Sugar,	94,001	169,662
Ixtle,	349,537	694,922
Coffee,	8,104,302	12,670,783
Hard woods,	2,688,811	4,200,880
Lead,	1,572,402	3,124,779

Total value of exported minerals, 1895	$52,535,854
Total value of exported minerals, 1896	64,838,596
Exportation of uncoined silver	26,000,000
Surplus revenue in the Federal Treasury, 1896	5,451,284
Total value of exports, 1896	105,016,905
Total value of imports, 1896	80,182,582
Balance of trade or $2.00 per capita	24,834,320

COMPARISON OF EARNINGS OF THE MEXICAN CENTRAL RAILWAY FROM 1885 TO 1896, INCLUSIVE.

Year.	Miles Operated.	Gross Earnings.	Earnings per Mile Operated.
1885	1,235.90	$3,559,560.75	$2,858.50
1886	1,235.90	3,857,705.85	3,121.37
1887	1,235.90	4,886,578.67	3,710.06
1888	1,316.40	5,774,331.31	4,028.03
1889	1,461.85	6,337,225.38	4,009.83
1890	1,527.20	6,425,694.08	4,009.08
1891	1,665.11	7,374,538.02	4,169.54
1892	1,824.83	7,963,253.69	4,146.07
1893	1,846.64	7,981,768.31	4,322.32
1894	1,859.83	8,426,025.28	4,530.53
1895	1,859.83	9,495,865.68	5,105.77
1896	1,869.60	10,208,020.39	5,460.00

TITLES.

UNTIL recent years nearly all the desirable agricultural lands of Mexico have been held in large tracts by a comparatively small number of owners. The system of land ownership which prevailed here dates back to the subdivision of the lands of New Spain by the Spanish crown among the soldiers and adventurers who aided in conquest. Lands were for many years practically exempt from taxation.

Owing to the difficulty in effecting an exchange of commodities (as there were scarcely any facilities for transportation) and because of the unsettled condition of the country, each haciendado (proprietor) was compelled to rely almost entirely upon the products of his own estate for subsistence. Accordingly a large area of land was put under cultivation or otherwise utilized, in order that he might provide a sufficient variety and quantity of products for his enjoyment in time of peace, and also accumulate a surplus for his necessities in periods of internal disorder or whenever his crops might fail. The great haciendas of the country have remained for many generations in possession of the descendants of the original owners.

VAQUEROS (CATTLE COUNTRY)

Conditions are now very different from those of the olden time. The railroads have made transportation easy, cheap and safe. Exchange of products between districts is the order of the present day. Each hacienda can now be put wholly or chiefly to cultivating that for which it is best adapted, be it grain, fruit, cotton or sugar; and the proprietor of each hacienda can buy, cheaper than he can raise, such things as formerly he was compelled to cultivate. Hence they are now offering lands for sale which once they needed for their own use. Desirable properties can now be purchased in various districts of the republic at prices ranging from seventy-five cents and upward per acre.

The Spanish government early set aside certain defined sections of territory for the use of the Indian population of the country. These sections, called "Congregaciones," exist in nearly all the fertile subtropical districts. In these sections undeveloped lands can usually be bought in lots of ten acres and upward, to suit purchaser, for from one dollar to eight dollars per acre, Mexican money.

Titles to these lands are possessory, the fee simple being vested in a grant which is owned by the pueblo, or community. Transfer of title to these lands is made by a bill of sale acknowledged by the cacique (or chief) of the village. The title lapses through abandonment of the land or nonpayment of taxes, the land reverting to the pueblo. Many tracts of good land are held in "Condueñazgos," which are grants made by the King of Spain to *individuals*. These grants have never been subdivided by the heirs of the original owners, and are now owned by all of those heirs in common.

The purchaser of these lands buys an interest in the Condueñazgo. Practically the transaction is like buying shares in a stock company. The buyer has a right to take possession of any quantity of unoccupied land that he will fence.

In case of a future subdivision of the lands of the Condueñazgo (a division may be made at any time by agreement of stockholders representing a majority interest) the portion of each individual is made to correspond to the amount of stock which he owns; for example: the owner of one thousand dollars' worth of stock, who is in possession of two thousand dollars' worth of land, must let his excess land be divided, or he may pay into the general treasury of the Condueñazgo the difference between the value of his stock and the value of the land in his possession, and keep the land; that is, he has the first chance to buy the land at the set valuation on it. This valuation of his tract is, however, not increased by any improvements which he has made upon it.

Municipal lands are those which are owned by the various municipalities. Tracts of these municipal lands may be "denounced" (or "claimed," as we say in the States,) by any one who will occupy it and will pay to the municipality the price set upon it. The deed is confirmed by the state government and becomes an absolute title. This land is forfeited by abandonment and by nonpayment of taxes. When forfeited it becomes again the property of the municipality, and may be "denounced" again.

The titles to church lands (lands which once belonged to the various Catholic organizations, and which the reform party, under President Juarez, "nationalized") are exactly like the titles to other government lands.

The titles of most of the large farms, or haciendas of Mexico, are perfect, being grants from the King of Spain confirmed by the Federal government.

It is always advisable for purchasers to submit the matter of title to some reliable real estate lawyer, who is thoroughly conversant with the subject and capable of giving an accurate opinion.

EDUCATION.

INCLUDING classes for instruction in the arts and trades there are in the republic 10,746 government schools. They have an average attendance of 545,000. Primary education is compulsory. There are also many private schools and colleges.

In the city of Mexico the Federal government maintains the following institutions: Academy of Fine Arts, School of Civil Engineering, School of Medicine, Law School, Academy of Commerce, Academy of Arts and Trades, Conservatory of Music, Military College, School of Mines, two Normal Schools for teachers of both sexes, also schools for the deaf, for the dumb, and for the blind. In the various states there are many similar institutions supported by the state governments. Mexico annually expends between four million and five million dollars for the education of her people.

There are seventy-two public libraries in the country. The National Library at the capital contains 265,000 volumes. At the present time Mexico issues about 350 periodical publications, including the daily and weekly newspapers, also magazines, literary reviews and organs of the various industries and interests.

CAUSES OF PROSPERITY.

WHILE Mexico's prosperity is unquestionably due to a large number of causes, prominent among which are the suppressions of disorder, the extension of railroads, and the liberal policy of the government towards foreign capitalists and emigrants, it is very evident that her industrial growth has been powerfully stimulated by the existing monetary standard.

When silver and gold as valued in the world's commodities parted company, and Mexican dollars (which were being exported to Europe) were sold for a less price as measured in the currency of the gold standard countries, a rise in the price of all imported articles begun in Mexico. From this time dates the development of Mexico's cotton and woolen industries, as well as the increase in the exportation of articles other than precious metals. The demand and the margin of profit for home-made goods increased as Mexican dollars depreciated. The native manufacturer enlarged his operations, introduced improved machinery, and began to compete successfully with many grades of imported goods.

The consumer now purchases from the Mexican manufacturer at the same price in silver as when silver was at par with gold, instead of being exported to Europe as formerly. Many millions of dollars have thus been kept at home and added to the capital of the country.

Cotton mills have been constructed in all parts of the republic. The acreage of cotton is constantly increasing, but the native crop is not yet sufficient to supply the demand, and large quantities of cotton are imported from the United States.

The history of the woolen trade has been almost identical with that of cotton.

The Mexican manufacturer of woolens produces now a very good article, although he cannot yet compete with the finer fabrics of France and England. In former years there was a considerable exportation of wool to the United States; now there is a considerable importation of it from the United States into Mexico.

While it is true that the Mexican dollar, as measured in francs, marks, or pounds sterling, has decreased in value nearly fifty per cent, it is also true that prices of almost every class of foreign goods have also decreased fifty per cent. A suit of clothes made from the finest quality of imported goods costs only the same number of Mexican silver dollars today that it cost twenty-five years ago.

Note also the effect on real estate. Coffee plantations have risen in value from $75 or $80 an acre, the price when gold was at par with silver, to $200 to $800 an acre. The annual profits of these plantations have risen from $10 or $15 an acre, to from $50 to $150 an acre. Similar advances are true also in sugar and tobacco haciendas.

The premium on gold has been the cause of immense internal improvements throughout the country. The capital kept at home has been invested in irrigation schemes, in improving large tracts of fallow land, and in other enterprises of a like character. The premium has also brought much foreign capital here which has been invested in various branches of industry, particularly in the production of articles for exportation.

The foreign investor doubles his capital when he brings it to Mexico. He gets the advantage of cheap and docile labor for silver, and sells his exported product for gold.

This great stimulation to all industrial enterprises, the building of railroads, the establishment of factories, and the cultivation of

OCOTLAN, NEAR LAKE CHAPALA

new thousands of acres of land—all these have had a notable effect upon the people. The great demand for labor has benefitted them immensely, and has promoted peace and prosperity throughout the country.

The resources and opportunities of Mexico have only been recently revealed to her own people as well as to foreigners. It is much easier now than it ever was before, to get capital here at a relatively low rate of interest for any legitimate enterprise, because, first, there is more money in the country than when we were importing so largely; and because, second, the business man is willing, under present conditions, to take risks which would be considered too great in an era of low prices and a contracted currency.

The native producer has prospered under silver at the expense of the foreign merchant and of the importer. Silver in Mexico has stimulated exports and contracted imports.

THE SPORTSMAN'S PARADISE.

ALTHOUGH game is found along almost the entire line of the Mexican Central Railway, local conditions are such that certain districts offer greater inducements than others to the sportsman.

The stations of Yurecuaro, La Barca, and Ocotlan on the Guadalajara Branch, are immediately contiguous to marshes which are the winter resort of every kind of aquatic bird from snipe to swan. There is probably no other place in the Americas where so many wild fowl congregate. Pelican, swan, geese, brant, ducks of every variety, snipe, curlew and sand-hill cranes are found here in immense numbers.

A favorite way of hunting ducks and geese is by stalking them from a canoe. The rushes render it easy to approach the feeding birds; the abundance and the tameness of the birds permit of stalking a large number of flocks in the course of a day. Point shooting, popular among sportsmen along the shores of Chesapeake Bay, may be enjoyed here, but it is more expensive, as it is necessary to have the natives fire little sky-rockets at the flocks to make them fly over the points.

This region is known as the Lake Chapala district It can be conveniently visited in connection with a very pleasant trip over our Guadalajara Branch. Guides and canoes can be easily obtained at any of the stations above named.

There is good deer hunting about Villar, east of San Luis Potosi, on the Tampico Branch, and also in the vicinity of Jimulco on the main line.

About twenty miles south from San Bartolo, on the Tampico line are swamps formed by the water from large springs. In these swamps in the winter season great numbers of aquatic birds are found. To the south are mountains in which deer, wild hogs and an occasional Mexican lion are seen. The true paradise of the sportsman lies further east on the Tampico line, in the foothills between the mountains and the gulf. Here almost every kind of game is found abundant. The alligator and the manitee may be seen along the rivers near the gulf; in the mountains are panthers, tigers, and wild hogs; in the hills are countless pheasants, of which there are here five varieties, varying from the size of a pigeon to that of a turkey. Guides can be procured, but they speak only Spanish.

In the vicinity of Tampico there is probably the finest sea fishing on the gulf, if not the finest on the whole Atlantic coast. In the river Panuco the tarpon, the pargo, and the curel are caught by trolling, by still fishing, by spearing, and occasionally with the fly. There is good beach fishing from the jetties. This jetty fishing is similar to shumming as practiced on the shores of Long Island Sound for sea bass. Here fish weighing from four ounces to seventy-five pounds may be hooked. A few miles from the mouth of the Panuco are the red snapper banks, where the fish are large and very abundant.

In the little streams and rivers which thread the tropical forests of this region, muscovy duck hunting is to be had. The birds are large, brilliant in plumage, and fine for eating.

There is no "closed season" in Mexico; shooting is allowable at any time of year. Tourists and sportsmen can bring to Mexico their own guns and a limited quantity of ammunition free of all duties.

A SAFE AND PROFITABLE INVESTMENT.

CAREFUL observers confirm the truth of the statement often repeated by the late General Butler, that "the surest, safest, quickest, and most honest way to get rich is by judicious investment in real estate." The judicious purchase of subtropical land is not a speculative investment. A large return from such an investment is as certain as anything in the future can be. Hard times do not lessen the productiveness of a fertile soil, nor do financial storms affect a mild and even climate.

The United States affords the greatest market in the world for subtropical fruits and other products, but she can raise within her borders only a fraction of what she consumes. Mexico, her next-door neighbor, is bound to be the chief source of supply for her increasing demand.

The quantity of land, even in Mexico, that is available for the exporting fruit culturist is not unlimited ; in fact it is quite limited. Profits in this business absolutely depend upon conditions which are not enjoyed by all the fertile tracts of Mexico, and which until within a few years were not enjoyed by any of them. These conditions, in addition to a mild climate and a fertile soil, are, first, a demand for the product ; and second, a quick delivery to market. There has always been quite a demand, but now it is greater than ever and is constantly increasing. The chief obstacle to success in exporting these perishable products from Mexico was a lack of quick transportation. This obstacle is now happily removed, so far as lands within easy and quick reach of the railroad are concerned. Suitable lands sufficiently accessible to lines of transportation, we repeat, are quite limited. Whoever secures these lands secures the market for oranges, lemons, bananas and pineapples, which are perishable products and cannot endure delay in delivery.

Now is the time for the investor and fruit raiser to secure these lands. Their prospective value is very high, their present price is very low, their profitableness seems to be assured beyond a doubt. A small capital, with plenty of energy and pluck, will here make for anyone a snug little fortune.

The improvements of Tampico harbor and the recent extensions of railroads have made easily accessible to market a region admirably adapted to this fruit industry. This region tributary to the Tampico Branch has been described somewhat in detail in the previous pages (see pages 13-15).

This Huasteca region is one of the sections which we commend to the attention of the investor.

Another section which offers fine opportunities to the investor and the fruit raiser is the country along the Guadalajara Branch in the state of Jalisco. Both these sections have a climate unsurpassed by that of any other part of Mexico.

In considering the question of a land purchase here, and in figuring its probable profit, bear in mind this *very important* fact and factor: You pay Mexican silver for Mexican land and labor, and you are paid in gold for whatever you export from Mexico.

WHO SHOULD SETTLE IN MEXICO.

ANY one who has capital, say at least two thousand dollars (in American money), can settle in this country with a well-founded hope of success. With this sum he can buy and properly equip for production land enough to soon *earn* him a comfortable home. Plenty of the best of labor is at hand and is cheap. The man who comes to Mexico to live or to invest must *produce* if he is to make his way. He *must make* something that will sell, and that will sell for more than it costs him, if he is to have a profit for his capital and his work. The sooner he gets a knowledge of the prevailing language of the country, the Spanish, the better for him. The sooner he accepts or adapts himself to the manners and customs of the country the better for him. There are the best of reasons for many things here which seem strange to a foreigner, which reasons, in due time, a residence in the country will reveal. The man who is to succeed in Mexico must *learn* as well as teach; he must be gentle as well as forceful. Kindness will double his capital so far as native labor is concerned.

There is abundant opportunity here for any one who with capital, large or small, with energy and prudence, will engage in *any* of the enterprises which have been mentioned; and any one who can not bring with him these essential items, had better stay where he is until he can acquire them. There is no use in discounting disappointment in Mexico or anywhere else. The laws of "success" are the same here as elsewhere. Excellent opportunities are offered here to all who know and abide by those laws, and *no chance at all* for those who do not. Mexico offers no inducement to foreigners who have no capital but labor of some kind, unless it be to *a few* who can speak Spanish and who are familiar with the customs of the Mexican people. Hard times in gold standard countries have caused many mechanics, carpenters, painters, printers, clerks, trainmen, etc., to come to Mexico in search of employment. Nearly all have been disappointed, and only those in any line of work are or will be wanted who will be of *immediate* use to the employer. A foreigner who will give the subject a moment's thought will readily understand some of the difficulties with which he will have to contend in seeking employment among a people whose character and language are different from his own. The difficulty is vastly increased where, as here, the home supply of manual labor greatly exceeds the demand.

Most of our railroads are required by government, in return for privileges granted them, to employ native help in certain capacities. In addition to this, many positions can be filled only by Mexicans. Thus the number of openings in railroad employment available to foreigners is very small; and at the present time all vacancies can be easily filled from the supply of unemployed artisans already on the ground.

In this connection we present some remarks of the United States Minister to Mexico, Ex-Senator Ransom, on the general subject of settlement in Mexico. He says:

Very many people have been to see me or have written to me about settling or investing in Mexico. I have invariably told them that Mexico is a wonderful country, possessing an equable and mild climate, and very fertile lands where there is rain or irrigation; that tropical fruits abound; but that there is only one safe rule for intending investors or settlers to follow, which is to see well for themselves, to look before they leap. They should examine and consider everything connected with their settlement or investment. Above all, they should take sufficient time for their observations. I have cautioned all who intended settling in the country, and who lacked experience, to examine the question of titles with the greatest care, to obtain the best legal advice in reference to them, and also to look well into the all-important matters of health, water, labor and crops; in short, to become thoroughly conversant with the salient features of the part of the country they proposed to make their home. I have told them that unless they did this, they would in all probability be doomed to disappointment. I have never omitted to make mention of the fact that Mexico is improving every day; that she has an excellent administration of the government; that confidence as to its stability is everywhere on the increase. I have done this because I fear that misrepresentations made in the United States by interested persons may delude many people into coming here. It is absolutely essential to success that a man intending to move to Mexico should spare the time to come and see what he contemplates doing before he does it. The labor of Mexico is fairly good. There is a large field here for profitable enterprises. Many Americans who have come here have made large fortunes. Many other Americans have met with disappointments and failures. While there are opportunities here for skilled labor, there are practically none for unskilled labor, inasmuch as the latter cannot survive the competition existing here. The labor of Mexico is more abundant and much cheaper than that of the United States.

THE VALLEY OF THE LERMA.

WE give this name, for convenience, to that extensive region which is served by and is tributary to the Guadalajara Branch of the Mexican Central Railway. We wish to call especial attention to this region, for it is justly regarded by many as "the jewel of Mexico." The river Lerma is the Mississippi of

Mexico. Its length from its source to San Blas, where it empties into the Pacific ocean, is fully 450 miles. Below Lake Chapala it is given on some maps the name of "Rio Grande de Santiago," and on others the name "Lerma" is correctly given to the whole stream from source to mouth. Because it flows for a few miles through the eastern end of Lake Chapala, it should not lose its name, as it does not lose itself in the lake. Its course can be distinctly traced across the lake by the color of its water. The lake is really an overflow reservoir made by the Lerma in its course to the ocean, and is not the source of another river. Lerma let it be from mountain to sea.

The Mexican Central's branch to Guadalajara follows this Lerma valley for 150 miles. This part of the valley may be called correctly "the granary and the garden of Mexico." Some reference has been made in our remarks on "orange culture" (page 34) to the "garden" features, and in the notice of the Bajio (pages 16 and 20) mention is made of the "granary" capacity of the eastern end of this region. Here we speak more in detail of the valley west of La Barca. We are here on the great Central Plateau, although in a valley. At no point in this region are we below an elevation of five thousand feet above sea level. The climate is all that can be desired; the scenery is charming, although not grand. One is constantly reminded of the New England hill country; only the villages, the haciendas, the costumes and the customs of the people make the observer realize that he is in Mexico. Says a lady who has just returned from a tour of observation: "I have traveled over four thousand miles in Mexico, and of all sections that I have seen I think the Lerma valley between La Barca and Guadalajara is the most attractive. If I ever go to Mexico to live, my home shall be somewhere in this section of the valley, where I can take, with only a short journey, a look at the Mexican Niagara, can have an occasional excursion on the Mexican Lake George, and can run often into the Mexican Paris." Nowhere else in the republic can one find such a variety of beautiful scenery, mountain, river and lake, so convenient to a large city, as in the section which this lady mentions.

Climate and scenery, however, will not suffice to provide for the lady (who evidently has an eye for the beautiful) shopping money and funds with which to go often to Guadalajara, the "Paris of Mexico," or to visit the Falls of Juanicatlan, or to take trips upon Lake Chapala. But the region is noted not alone for its climate and its charming scenery: it has *a world-wide renown for its fertile soil.* The state of Jalisco annually produces about eighteen million bushels of corn, three million bushels of wheat, and a million bushels of beans, a large proportion of which must be credited to the Lerma valley.

Whoever wishes to engage in the production of these staple crops, or in any of the branches of agriculture except those which require a tropical climate, will do well to visit and *study* this section of the Lerma valley between La Barca and Guadalajara.

GUADALAJARA

IS the second city in the republic in population and perhaps the first in beauty. The capital is much larger, and is called by some the most beautiful capital in the world; but there are people who think Guadalajara is more beautiful than the City of Mexico. One thing is certain: the existence of such a magnificent city as is Guadalajara, in the far interior of the country, is proof of the richness of the surrounding country. The fertility of the valleys and the wealth of the mountains of Jalisco account for the presence and prosperity of this city, which (founded in 1535) today by its thrift astonishes and by its beauty charms every visitor. It is the capital of Jalisco, one of the wealthiest states of the Mexican Union, and a state which, perhaps, is making more rapid progress in the development of its resources than any other. It is a good state for an American or for any enterprising foreigner to settle in.

LAKE CHAPALA

IS the largest lake in Mexico, being fifty miles long, and from ten to twenty miles wide. A steamer leaves Ocotlan every Tuesday and Friday for a trip round the lake. The principal village of this little inland sea is Chapala, where there are some

VIEW ON LAKE CHAPALA

famous hot springs. This is the resort which is most convenient to Guadalajara, and it receives considerable patronage. The steamer will make it more easily accessible than it formerly was, and doubtless will greatly increase the patronage of Chapala Springs. No more charming excursion for a lover of fine scenery can be found in all Mexico than this trip round Lake Chapala. This vicinity is well worth the attention of any one who wants to find a good place for the establishment of a sanitarium or a pleasure resort.

TAMPICO AND VICINITY.

NOWHERE else on the Atlantic coast of America has there been wrought within the last ten years so marvelous a change as at Tampico. No one can appreciate the improvements there so thoroughly as those who go down to the sea in ships, who do business in great waters, and especially those who have been accustomed to do business at the so-called ports of the Gulf of Mexico.

Where, a few years ago, there was only a shallow roadstead, dangerous for shipping because of exposure to the notorious norther, there is now the safest port on the gulf. American enterprise has moved from the mountains, more than seventy miles away, a half million tons of rocks to the sea, has piled them into two walls, which, a thousand feet apart, extend seven thousand feet into the gulf; has, between these walls, deepened the channel from the sea into the river by cutting through the bar, and thus has made a passage for the largest vessels of commerce into a smooth and land-locked harbor. On the city front, seven miles up the Panuco from the sea, are ample wharves at which ship and rail are brought together, where goods are loaded and discharged as carefully and as expeditiously as they are in New York or Boston.

Because of its safety, its depth of water, and its superior facilities for loading and discharging cargo, Tampico has already become the chief port of the republic. The following figures concerning the business done at Tampico and Vera Cruz in 1895 and 1896 are interesting, and tell their own story. The figures are taken from the official report of the Department of Finance for the fiscal year ending June 30, 1896.

Tonnage which passed through the port of Tampico in 1896	1,038,993 tons
Tonnage which passed through the port of Vera Cruz in 1896	402,329 tons
Value of imports, Tampico, 1895	$3,642,007
" " " " 1896	8,685,442
Value of exports, Tampico, 1895	15,543,228
" " " " 1896	23,920,464
Value of imports, Vera Cruz, 1895	16,123,505
" " " " " 1896	15,696,544
Value of exports, Vera Cruz, 1895	27,413,009
" " " " " 1896	22,354,298

The principal articles passing through the port of Tampico are ixtle, fustic, hides, sarsaparilla, honey, cedar and silver lead bullion.

Extensive harbor improvements are now being made which will be of the greatest value to the port of Tampico. A new Custom House Building, a wharf and other facilities for the despatch of business are now in process of construction by the government. The Custom House will be a substantial, fire-proof structure 984 feet long and 151 feet wide. It will be equipped with all the improved devices for handling goods.

The wharf, 1,148 feet long and 49 feet wide, will extend into the river so that vessels of 24 feet draught can be moored alongside.

When these improvements, which will cost about $1,500,000, are completed, Tampico will have the largest and best equipped Custom House and wharf in the republic, and the consequent advantage which will accrue to vessels in the prompter despatch, as compared with that of other ports, will no doubt bring a large amount of shipping to Tampico and give a great impetus to the port.

The Waters-Pierce Oil Company, recognizing this place as the best distributing point, has removed its refinery from San Luis

-Potosi to Tampico. The establishment will give employment to between two and three hundred men. This company will also construct a new wharf.

Mexican capitalists contemplate establishing a large cold storage plant at Tampico. The plan of the company is to ship cattle to Tampico by rail, slaughter them there, and export the beef to Europe in vessels adapted to the trade. The packing and shipping of fish to the interior of the country has been tried in an experimental way, and the result justifies the extension of the industry.

Tampico is the port nearest to and in most direct communication with interior cities and the great mining camps of the republic. Its facilities for loading and unloading freight far surpass those of any other Mexican port. Its volume of business will constantly increase.

Immediately tributary to Tampico is the beautiful and fertile Huasteca region, the paradise of the farmer, the stockman and the horticulturist. This region, which we have spoken of at some length in previous pages, has hardly begun to show what it can do. Notwithstanding its great natural advantages, only a very small fraction of it has been brought under cultivation. A few scattered villages, here and there a ranch, an occasional coffee patch, a few orange and lemon groves and small plots of corn, beans and tobacco may be seen there, but they merely show the possibilities of this favored region. We only repeat here what we have said about this section of country when we say that the Huasteca offers some of the finest opportunities for money making that can be found in Mexico.

Mileage of the Mexican Central Railway.

Main Line, City of Mexico to Ciudad Juarez	1,224.16
Santiago Branch, City of Mexico to Santiago	1.40
Pachuca Branch, Tula to Pachuca	43.81
Guanajuato Branch, Silao to Marfil	11.56
Guadalajara Branch, Irapuato to Guadalajara	161.21
Ameca Extension, Guadalajara to Ameca	55.41
San Luis Division, Chicalote to Tampico	406.93
Branch to Compañia Metalúrgica Mexicana Smelter San Luis Potosi	5.19
Bar Extension, Tampico to La Barra	6.21
Laguna Extension, Lerdo to San Pedro	39.78
Total	1,955.66

THE following agents of the Mexican Central Railway Company, Limited, will, on application, furnish freight and ticket rates, and answer inquiries in regard to Mexico:

A. HOFFMAN,
General Freight and Passenger Agent,
City of Mexico.

W. D. MURDOCK,
Assistant General Passenger Agent,
City of Mexico.

M. H. KING,
Western Agent,
236 South Clark Street,
Chicago, Ill.

W. C. CARSON,
Eastern Agent,
No. 1 Broadway, New York City.

·W. H. BATES,
Traveling, Freight and Pass. Agent,
236 South Clark Street,
Chicago, Ill.

F. J. BONAVITA,
Traveling, Freight and Pass. Agent,
No. 1 Broadway, New York City.

T. R. RYAN,
General Agent,
Carew Building, Cincinnati, Ohio.

J. H. SNOW,
Traveling, Freight and Pass. Agent,
Carew Building, Cincinnati, Ohio.

C. E. MINER,
Western Passenger Agent,
Houser Building, St. Louis, Mo.

H. E. KING,
Contracting Agent,
Houser Building, St. Louis, Mo.

J. F. DONOHOE,
Southern Agent,
404 Canal St., New Orleans, La.

R. E. COMFORT,
Commercial Agent,
El Paso, Tex.

W. G. WALTER,
General European Agent,
8A Rumford Pl., Liverpool, Eng.

A. V. TEMPLE,
Manager Bureau of Information,
City of Mexico.

www.ingramcontent.com/pod-product-compliance
Lightning Source LLC
Chambersburg PA
CBHW022143090426

42742CB00010B/1363